D0759802

Pebble®

Watch It Grow

Snails

by Martha E. H. Rustad

Consulting editor: Gail Saunders-Smith, PhD

Consultant: Paul Callomon, Collections Manager
Academy of Natural Sciences
Philadelphia, Pennsylvania

Capstone
press®

Mankato, Minnesota

Pebble Books are published by Capstone Press,
151 Good Counsel Drive, P.O. Box 669, Mankato, Minnesota 56002.
www.capstonepress.com

Library of Congress Cataloging-in-Publication Data
Rustad, Martha E. H. (Martha Elizabeth Hillman), 1975–
    Snails / by Martha E. H. Rustad.
    p. cm. — (Pebble books. Watch it grow)
    Includes bibliographical references and index.
    Summary: "Simple text and photographs present the life cycle of apple
snails" — Provided by publisher.
    ISBN: 978-1-4296-3308-6 (library binding)
    ISBN: 978-1-4296-3854-8 (paperback)
    1. Snails — Life cycles — Juvenile literature. I. Title. II. Series.
QL430.4.R87 2010
594'.3 — dc22   2009004918

Note: This book tells about apple snails, a kind of freshwater snail. The photographs show the life cycle of apple snails.

Note to Parents and Teachers

The Watch It Grow set supports national science standards related to life science. This book describes and illustrates apple snails. The images support early readers in understanding the text. The repetition of words and phrases helps early readers learn new words. This book also introduces early readers to subject-specific vocabulary words, which are defined in the Glossary section. Early readers may need assistance to read some words and to use the Table of Contents, Glossary, Read More, Internet Sites, and Index sections of the book.

Table of Contents

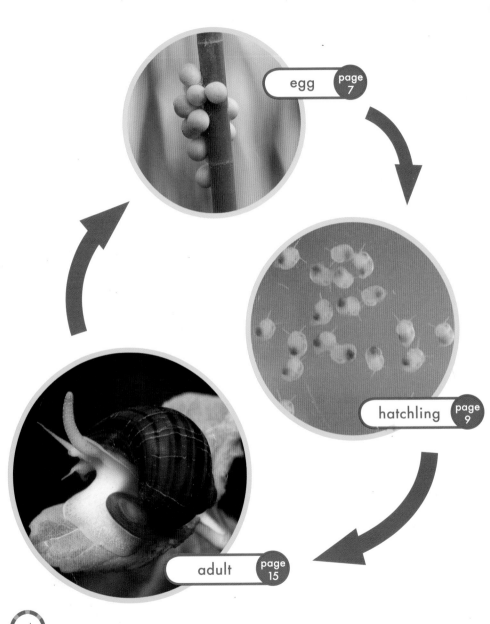

egg page 7

hatchling page 9

adult page 15

What Are Snails?

Snails are invertebrates.
They have a soft body
and a hard shell.
Apple snails live in water.
They change as they grow.

egg

From Egg to Hatchling

Apple snails begin life
as tiny eggs.
Most apple snails lay eggs
outside the water
on plants or rocks.

After about two weeks,
the snail eggs hatch.
The hatchlings look like
tiny adult snails.
Their shells are thin.

Hatchlings enter the water.

They eat and eat.

They eat plants
and algae.

The shells of hatchlings become thicker.
Their shells grow bigger as their bodies grow.

From Hatchling to Adult

Hatchlings become adults
after several months.
Adults can mate
and lay eggs.

tentacle

foot

An apple snail's head
and foot stick out of its shell.
Its tentacles, eyes, and mouth
are on its head.
A snail uses its foot to move.

Apple snails carry their shells on their backs.
The shell is like a house.
Snails pull their bodies inside their shells to stay safe.

Adult snails keep growing.
Rings appear on their shells
as they grow.
Most apple snails live
three to four years.

Glossary

algae — small plants without roots or stems that grow in water

foot — a body part on which an invertebrate stands or moves; a snail moves with its foot.

hatch — to break out of an egg

hatchling — a young animal that has just come out of its egg

invertebrate — an animal without a backbone

mate — to join together to produce young

shell — a hard outer covering; shells protect snails and give them shelter.

tentacle — a thin, flexible arm on some animals; snails have two or four tentacles on their heads.

Read More

Murray, Peter. *Snails*. New Naturebooks. Chanhassen, Minn.: Child's World, 2007.

White, Nancy. *Creeping Land Snails*. No Backbone! The World of Invertebrates. New York: Bearport, 2009.

Internet Sites

FactHound offers a safe, fun way to find Internet sites related to this book. All of the sites on FactHound have been researched by our staff.

Here's all you do:

Visit *www.facthound.com*

FactHound will fetch the best sites for you!

Index

Word Count: 170
Grade: 1
Early-Intervention Level: 21

Editorial Credits
Katy Kudela, editor; Alison Thiele, designer; Marcie Spence, media researcher

Photo Credits
Alamy/Arco Images GmbH, 14; Chris Johnson, cover (eggs), 4 (top), 6 (inset);
    Juniors Bildarchiv, 16; Maximilian Weinzierl, cover (apple snail)
Courtesy of Jedi Kim, cover (hatchlings), 4 (middle), 8
Courtesy of Robert Pilla, 10, 12
Getty Images Inc./Melissa Farlow/National Geographic, 6
Peter Arnold/Reinhard, H., 4 (bottom), 20
Visuals Unlimited/Inga Spence, 1, 18